DEAR DREAMER

DEAR DREAMER

NIHAR SHARMA

www.SharmaNihar.com

www.facebook.com/thedreamerdiary

www.instagram.com/thedream_diary

www.twitter.com/thedream_diary

ISBN: 0-9983811-1-X

ISBN-13: 978-0-9983811-1-4

Cover and interior illustrations by Katarzyna Surman.

To new beginnings.
To being stronger than I was before.
To dreams and hopes and love
and laughter.
To the spring this winter hides inside it.
To overcast skies and the sun
always shining behind them.
A toast.
To the me I am slowly becoming.
And to you,
for you have helped me arrive here.

CONFUSION

\#1

I
yearn
to
tell you
how
terrified
I am.

But
would
you
still
love me

after?

2

Her tiny fingers tie the ends of the rag in a knot around her neck, and she transforms into one of the super heroes she often reads about, running and skipping in the garden as the makeshift cape flows behind her in the wind. And then, in a blink, she changes into a royal princess, or a young queen, with her cloak slowly trailing behind her as she walks gracefully through her castle. Yet sadly, times change, and it is just a matter of years, when the cloth no longer serves as a portal to her dreams, but instead, she finds herself caged within it. Ordered to cover her head with it, to drape it over her body, to hide herself inside, she stifles in the confinement, suffocated and restrained, struggling to breathe, to tread freely, to fly, confused and terrified, wondering, how something, that denoted so much freedom, has suddenly become her prison, and why, that which gave her wings, has somehow ended up clipping them?

3

Some days
she would get lost
in the pages of a book
as though the ink itself
flowed through her veins
her heart beat echoed
the highs and the lows
and the life of each character
hung to the branches
of her spine
she would laugh with
their triumphs
weep with their loss
and if, suddenly
someone pulled her out
to the real world
her eyes would take time
to adjust to the bleak colours
her ears would not
accept the noise
and her heart
would sink
as she realized
where she was

and that
she did not belong there.

#4

Her mornings
carry
 inhibitions
and the struggles
to just be.
Her sunsets hold
blank pages
and
 infinite
possibilities.

#5

Some days
I sit at the table
and wonder
if parallel universes
can collide
and that
everyone else who sits there
is actually in
an alternate universe
talking about things
I have long lost
the want to make sense of.

#6

I have often
found myself
falling in love
with people's scars
and their dreams
and sometimes
the courage
they show
to sustain both.

7

She keeps her heart in a box
that has a one way road
she pours in her feelings
and purges all her loads,
she has a keen eye
and sees a little more
the sighs behind their smiles
the tears behind their doors,
she picks up their burdens
and puts them in the box
some have sharpened pieces
and some are jagged rocks,
these pinch and tear her heart
but she's too busy saving theirs
the pain begins to rise
yet she tries not to care,
one day she stops and cries
feeling helpless for the world
they watch her in confusion
as she lies bowed and curled,
then she pulls out the box
and shows them her wounded heart
they turn away disgusted
noticing all the broken parts,
and so she suffers in silence
for her voice was never heard
and they label her 'too sensitive'
like it is a bad word.

#8

There are
too many
of us
who
want to be
seen,
heard and
understood

and
too few
who take
the time to
listen,
observe
and accept.

#9

And you assume you know her
when all that you were shown
was this blanket of a skin
which covers her fragile bones,
you have not gazed within her heart
or waited patiently for her mind
to give you a slight glimpse
into the world which grows inside,
you have not sensed the
unsteady rhythm of her pulse
anytime she stumbles upon
something she loves,
neither watched the light
in her eyes grow dim
and see her veins darken
with the sorrow that swims,
nor have you heard the melodies
that burst forth from her core
when she finds a day worth living
and her spirit soars,
and you certainly have not felt
the nail imprints inside her palm
every time she barely manages
to control her inner storm.

#10

So
easy
to
fall
in
love
with,

          so
          very
          difficult
          to
          love.

#11

What is my conviction
but mere, frivolous
fantasies?
Dreams born out
of miseries,
solace found in
the madness,
wings stained with
rust from
the bars of a cage,
life found
 at the edge
of life itself.

#12

Ever felt so torn apart
like there is more
than one person living
inside you? So many
moods in the span of a
few seconds. Teenage
emotions trying to burst
out of an adult body.
Regrets for the chances
youth was too scared
to take. Yearnings for the
childhood that never
was.

#13

How often have we been
driven into the dark
by the weight
of our own insecurities
letting people define
every single aspect
of a life
they have never lived.

#14

Forgive me if I've
changed and you miss
the person you thought
you knew. I got lost
somewhere along the way
and the only fragments
worth saving were
insignificant pieces of
myself that I had not
bothered showing the
world anyway.

#15

And I am gone
I'm not sure where I went
I've tried looking in all the places
I used to frequent,
but I can't find myself
no matter how much I search
that circle of friends
the old school with the church,
that garden ledge
the faded couch in the hall
the wooden bookshelf
the mirror on the wall,
they never noticed I left
never asked to visit again
now footsteps replaced with
the quiet scribbling of a pen,
I search for the words
that will tell me of home
and if I made it there
because I am gone,
I didn't leave an address
and I'm not sure where I went
I've tried looking in all the places
I used to frequent.

#16

Do you see
my hands tremble
with longing for
a place to rest?

They have been
bleeding too long.

REALIZATION

She was a fool to build
her world on books,
walking through paper
towns that might crumble
any day. But she learnt
to live in them.
And that is what mattered.
She learnt to live.

#18

To find freedom
in solitude
is one of life's
greatest gifts.
To find comfort
in the written word
is one of life's
treasures.
They warn you
to get not too fond
of worldly possessions,
but this is my heart
that beats
within these pages.

#19

I think madness
is the soul
fighting to survive
and cling
to all that
it finds comfort in.

#20

Why do we fear
revealing ourselves?
Why is it so difficult
to find acceptance
within those we love?
And so we continue to
live this dual life
and it's crazy
how easy it has become.

#21

Whenever it rains
I swear I can almost
hear the earth
sighing with relief
weary of all the
burdens we have
thrown upon it.
Mothers are tough
but they are fragile too.
Their children are their
strength but also
sometimes their undoing.

#22

Why is the craving for
escape so great, that even
when we run and run and
run and never once find
ourselves home, we're still
tempted to walk the same
path over and over again,
maybe trying to stumble
upon something we might
have missed the first time
some point of no return with
no looking back, no coming
back. But all we do is run,
look back and come back.
Like going in circles, legs
tired, eyes forlorn, never
once finding what they are
searching for.

I hope you find yourself
soon.

#23

Often it is, that we feel
terribly insecure with our own
identity and cannot bear being
with ourselves. Laugh in
solitude and they will label
you insane, and so we crave
company to justify contentment.
The joke has worth only if it
finds approval from the group.
You have the right skin colour
only if the world thinks you
do. And maybe this is how
depression seeps in. We get so
exhausted trying to make people
love us
   when all we had to do was
   love ourselves.

#24

The still lake sleeps
dreaming of being the
perennial stream. It
waits each day for the
wind to swivel it around,
not knowing it itself
has the power to break
boundaries. For if it
keeps pushing the frontiers
again and again, one day
the dam will burst.

#25

So often have we heard the
words 'not good enough'
that they become an antidote
to the fear of shining too
brightly, of breaking our
own expectations and
becoming a person we do
not recognize. And every
night when distant dreams
and hopes torture us in our
sleep, we turn the other way
and sing these words to
ourselves like a lullaby,
we are not good enough.

If
mirrors
reflected
character
how many
of us
would find
the courage
to look
into
ourselves
every
single day?

They say the pain goes,
wounds heal, scars fade,
and how often have I
uttered the same words
to myself and to you?
Yet sometimes, this voice
feels so hollow, empty
of belief, and I watch
the syllables slip and
scatter on to the floor
trudged upon by these
weary feet.
My thoughts have a tendency
to lie to me, and now and
then they break my heart.

#28

And sometimes the scars stay
serving as a reminder
of what was almost lost
yet reclaimed.

29

There was a rock inside her chest and it
grew heavier everyday. She tried to lift it
out, but the world kept pushing it back in,
trying to convince her that it was a part
of her and that she herself was stone; rigid,
plain, featureless, waiting to be chiselled
in whichever form they so desired. Yet she
had heard the music of the streams and
bathed in the spray. Gushing, shimmering,
overflowing, it teased her and she slowly
felt herself turn lighter. She realized that
the river was gradually cutting through the
rock, and soon boundless infinitesimal
pieces of her became a part of the water and
it took her away. You can still hear her
voice in the chorus of the cascades and
watch her dance with the rhythm of the rapids.
Her laughter resounds through nature.
She is herself now, and no longer holds to
any definition but her own. You may find her
swirling in the wilderness, seeking other
rocks to free.

30

The universe
whispered to me
that night,

'do not fear pain
for I am built by it,
through it.'

#31

Often I have found
myself spellbound
under the night sky,
listening to the stars
talk in excited voices
about realms unknown
and some, in sweet,
low whispers, sing
beautiful lullabies.
There is a sense of peace
that courses through
my veins and I can almost
hear my heart humming
back to the heavens
that we are part of
something much bigger
than ourselves, and
no matter the hurdles,
no matter how down you feel
somehow I know,
that there is a little
magic that exists
in each of our lives,
if we only remember
 to look up.

Most of us carry a
piece of our personal
hell with us wherever
we go. And then I
wonder, why didn't it
occur to anyone to
carry heaven too?
Maybe that someone is
me. Maybe I'm going to
try carrying a bit of
heaven in my pockets
today.

I got tired of waiting
for better things to
come along. So I picked
up a pen and decided to
put down all the bad
parts and then make up
a happy ending, to perhaps
try and taste what that
would feel like. And I
think once you write
down a merry end, once
you create it in a corner
of your head, you're giving
permission to your heart
to believe that something
like that is possible. And
maybe that's the toughest
part, to have faith in what
seems so improbable.
Maybe that's what makes
all the difference.

#34

And suddenly one
morning she woke up
to find every object
touched with colour,
every sound- music,
and even silence had
a rhythm that she
could dance to.

35

She wasted so many days
trying to run away into
the void, hating this world
and all that humanity had
to offer. Most days when she
woke up and looked into
the mirror, all she could
see were two dead ends.
Some mornings she didn't
want to wake up at all.

And then what happened?

The voices in her head
told her a tale and she
grabbed a pen and re-wrote
her story. She became
her own fairy godmother
and knight in shining armor
and began to live in a place
where hurts could heal and
night welcomed day. She
started to love herself and
was her own prince charming.
She kissed herself awake.

ACCEPTANCE

#36

They say
she keeps her
head in the clouds
but maybe
the clouds come down
to protect
the worlds she holds
in her head.

#37

She holds
sunshine
in her arms
and the world
does not seem
like such a
dark place.

38

I discovered myself

from looking at all

the broken pieces

I'd let fall, and

never had I seen such

a beautiful mosaic.

#39

She wrote to escape reality
and suddenly stumbled upon one
she did not want escaping from.
And though she did not touch her
building blocks but they did not
make the same sense anymore.
Several new pathways had opened,
numerous old tunnels closed. And
she realized she may have lost
her way into her own soul. But
it was a good kind of loss. The
kind that surprises you. The kind
where you pick up a pen and it
reaches inside and hits dead ends
but also new beginnings. The kind
where you lose yourself, only to
be found, every day, in another way.

40

You want to be loved but you've
been running away my love, and
it's hard right now but it'll only
get harder tomorrow. And this path
that you've taken thinking you're
invisible to love and invincible
to love, this path runs right into
love. And if you were crazy enough
to map them all, you'd realize that
all paths do.

#41

You know those dreams
where there's something
chasing you and you keep
running and stumbling
through a maze? I have
been there often, trying
to escape the unseen.
But then I met you, and
I still found myself
running and stumbling,
yet suddenly, all the
directions began to make
sense and before I knew
it, I had found
 my way home.

42

There are going to be days
when I'm going to want to stand,
and there are going to be days
when I will want to crumble.
I hope you'll like to hold on
to all the broken pieces,
even the ones that hurt.
I hope you'll learn to love the
art of building me up again.

#43

Men, do not despair if you find it
difficult to understand a woman, for it
has been even tougher for her to
understand herself. When the world gives
you too many identities and not a single
one you can identify yourself with, it
becomes nearly impossible, a herculean
task, to sift through those layers and
find yourself. And when it has taken her
most of her lifetime, she must not keep
unfair expectations from you. She is a
walled structure; a multi-storey building
with many rooms. In each room, she has
placed a genuine piece of herself under
lock and key, for the world so often
wishes to break in and steal, destroy,
burn it all. And though she may have begun
to let you in, but all doors do not hold
the same key and some will only open when
you earn the trust of not attempting to
harm these carefully guarded fragments of
her soul. Till then you must create a home
in her living room. Till then she must let
you hold on to these misunderstandings
for a while.

#44

I hope that you wake up to a better morning
and the dreams you keep curled under your
pillow slip out and see the light of day.
I hope that you look in the mirror and find
someone familiar smiling back. I hope when
you sit alone the future beckons you more
than the past. I hope you get to stumble upon
a miracle. I hope you make a little time to
do what you truly love.

#45

You may hold joy in
your heart my love,
but you must also remember
to let pain walk through.
Pain reminds us what it is
like to feel. And to feel
is what makes us human.

46

I am sorry but
some days I have trouble
being the person
I promised to be.
Some days my old insecurities
come knocking back,
untying my shoe laces
and making me trip
on myself. You've been
teaching me to run
but times like these,
I fear walking.

#47

Dear Absence,

You said you'd just
come to visit but I
worry you've found a
home inside the hole
in my chest.
Maybe I fed you too
well. Maybe you never
mean to leave.

#48

Empty spaces
have a way
of spilling over
their emptiness
and sometimes
even the room
full of mirth
does not have
a place for her
to sit and rest
in.

#49

She is in love with
 Autumn
and all things falling;
falling,
            failing,
                    breaking,
and then picking the
pieces up,
romanticizing the
struggle to live,
rather than the act
of living itself.

50

I know you built a home
in your past, and you
find it too scary to
leave, even though all
that lies inside are
empty walls and broken
windows. You still linger,
hoping to find a way to
get it repaired, back in
shape. I know. Because I
linger in mine too.
Pain is our refuge.

#51

Of all the anger we let out, why
do we let it out on the wrong people?
There is great pain in rejection.
But I have come to realize the feelings
are not yours, the words are hearsay
which you end up repeating for you
do not have the courage to be vulnerable
anymore, so you push out everything
which twists itself out of place,
anything away from the ordinary,
the expected. It hurts you and you wish
to leave. Or let go. I wish there was
a way I could help you. I wish I
could tell you that you are strong,
and kind-hearted, and no matter
how cold you feel right now,
there is a warmth that radiates from
your being. I come searching for
that warmth. And I promise I won't try
to save you if you don't want to be saved.
Maybe it is I who needs the saving.
Please let me in..

Do not be so quick to judge,
my love. People become
who they are for life carves
them that way. You have not
stood where they stand, nor
fallen where they fell, neither
broken the same bones, the
same dreams, the same heart,
yet you allow yourself to decide
the existence they lead.
Let yourself be open-hearted for
a bit. Be patient. Be welcoming.
Be kind to someone today.

\#53

You can touch
to create a wound
or you can touch
to heal it
either way
the scars stay
but it is your choice
what memories
you leave with them.

Sometimes people begin
to slip away.
Where once your world
revolved around them,
you suddenly realize
that they have
slowly shifted to
the outskirts of your galaxy,
that it no longer matters
if the same sun
touches you both.
Where once you read them
in every word,
it somehow becomes tougher
to find words to remember them
with every passing day.
I guess, sometimes,
without even realizing,
 you begin to heal.
Sometimes, it begins to be okay.

\#55

Give it a rest.
Give yourself a rest.
Breathe.
Even nature lets itself
fall to pieces
for a while
until it has the strength
to rise up again.

56

One day it's going to be okay.
One day, all your broken pieces
are going to find their way home.
I know you think you've lost them,
just the way you think you've lost
yourself. It's like standing on a
small island in the middle of
the sea, not knowing how to
swim, yet always being tempted
to jump into the water and forget
all the sadness. You have a view
of the shore, but it's a very blurred
picture. And you don't think you'll
make it. But it's going to happen.
You'll jump into shallow pools
and learn how to paddle. Then
you'll jump into deeper ones, and
learn how to swim. One day, and
another, and another, till the
time you are strong enough.
And then you are going to dive
carefree, and before you know it,
you will have reached the other side.

57

Hope is stubborn.
It doesn't give
up on you even when
you give up on
yourself. You think
you've lost it, but
it just keeps
waiting around the
corner. Or it may
have lost its way
to you, but it still
sits somewhere with
that stubborn smile,
knowing
that you will get
through this.

#58

If you get to live a hundred lives

I hope you never lose your sense of

wonder and still stare at the stars

every night as though having seen them

for the first time.

#59

And one day, if all else fails
if the world around us begins to break
I hope you get to know me
the real me.
The one who hides out of sight
in fear she may not be good enough,
the one who loves fairy tales
rather than reality,
who spends her time
living in stories.
The one who when remembers your words,
recalls the tone of your voice
the light in your eyes,
the one who conceals herself in the day
and only peeks out at night
with no risk of being seen.

I hope one day you come looking
for the real me.
And I hope that day you like
what you see.

60

If she takes off her skin
would you be scared
of the world that grows within?
There are monuments
that her hopes and dreams
have built
and many that lie in rubble
which she hasn't yet found
the courage to clear.
Walk through the pieces with her.
Let not the stream of her thoughts
overwhelm you.
Step in it, bathe in it,
immerse yourself for a little while.
Do not try to hold her back
for she will slip through your fingers.
Dance together
to each of her graceful movements.
Fall in love with her music.

61

They know nothing of it
because they were never there
with you.
They just looked in from the outside,
from a distance, from afar,
not knowing, nor understanding,
what it felt to fall, to stay in
every day,
to not find a means to get out
and watch the world go by.
People ask you to come out
but no one gives you a ladder,
and even if they show you the rungs,
no one teaches you
how to climb them again.
I hope you find someone who does,
who isn't afraid to come down
or dirty their hands
building crevices into the walls
for you to lift yourself on,
who will hold you if you slip,
or at least be your motivation
to try again tomorrow.
Sometimes that someone comes
when you least expect them.
And if you are lucky enough
sometimes that someone is you.

62

I have tried to be a better person.
But there were days, even months,
where all I remember now is the
anger I felt towards myself, towards
all the desired traits people found
lacking in me. I have tried to change.
But the more I tried, the further I
went from what I knew. And it didn't
help. I only despised myself more,
for still hating the real me and failing
the fake me. So consumed I became
with hatred, that I cut off from both.
Vagrant, wanderer, lost, abandoned.
The real me knocked at my door, wanting
to come in, worried and anxious. The
fake one never came. And thus I knew.
I have tried to be a better person. But
the better person always lived inside me.

#63

Life is going to hold a lot of
twist and turns
and you're going to stumble and fall
and bleed and cry and then you're
going to get some thread
and sew yourself up.
There will be blind curves
and more than a few pits to sink into,
but promise me you'll keep your
head high, you won't give into the
temptation of caution,
of lowering your eyes and spending
all your living moments studying
the potholes in the road ahead.
Promise that you'll take time
to touch a flower
and maybe breathe into its scent,
and when the wind blows,
maybe just maybe you'll let
your hair flow, and if it rains
by god, if it rains, let it seep
into you, let it fill every vacant
space inside your body
and may you never feel
empty again.

64

Most days what keeps me going
is the courage and splendour that
exists in this world even for all
the pain it endures each day; to
find love in small things, value
in kindness, morality, simplicity,
and wonder. If you are reading this
know that you are beautiful. You
are beautiful for every random kind
act performed, every smile that has
brightened someone's day, every
little thought you are passionate
about. The songs you hum on lazy
mornings, the tiny twirl you take
when no one's watching, the tears
you try so hard to hide.
If I had to search for beauty, I
would look no further than the
twinkle in your eyes.

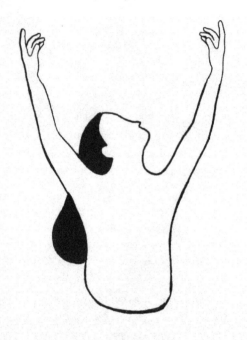

COURAGE

#65

She holds a lullaby
close to her chest.
A dream where
the earth is above
and the sky is down below
and when she lets go
she falls into the stars.
They wrap themselves
around her, and she sleeps
peacefully because
she's not scared
of falling anymore.

#66

I will never be
a crowd person.
I am too much
in love
with solitude
and I am afraid
it is too much
in love
with me too.

#67

There is
a peacefulness
to his fragrance,
so hard
to put into words.
A comfort
like none before.
A coming home
of sorts.

#68

I wonder if winter decided
to coat itself in white
to show to the world
that it is still beautiful,
that one should not fear it,
or run away from the
stark, dreary appearance
of withered trees and
decaying leaves.
Maybe, winter too, like us,
dreads abandonment.
Sometimes the ones
who feel the most unwanted
try the hardest.

Sometimes faith is
a fragile bird
and we put too much
hope on its wings.
We burden it down
with our wishing
and praying and yet
do nothing to
bolster its flight.
Sometimes we forget
to feed it.

She folds her arms
 close to her chest
  as though holding tightly
   all her pieces
    together in fear
     they may slip from her
      grasp and she may crumble.
He tries to hold her hand
 but her fingers
  do not relax. They are
   too used to their
    own grip, curling
     into themselves,
      firmly, tightly.
Her shoulders are stiff,
 they hurt but
  she keeps them that way
   for if she loosens
    her guard, they may
     drag her
      down.

Sometimes she is that weary.

71

Woman, beautiful is the neck they
praise, yet hang a noose around it
for every carefree step you take,
carved are the shoulders, drooping
too low from all the social burdens
hung upon them. Startling are the
eyes that peek through the veils of
secrecy.
They say it's for your protection.
Protection from whom? From them.
Because they are authoritative
enough to dictate your life yet
they cannot even dictate their own
libido. Sing a song for them but
hush do not scream, dance but do not
run. Your feet were chained from the
moment you learnt to stand on them.

But no more..

#72

She thinks about the things she cannot have.
And she wonders if it is okay to want,
to have a desire to speak up,
to yearn for a life worth living?
Will the world come folding down on her?
Will they hush her with their forbidding stares
and all the anger they own for reasons unknown?
Will she be able to walk the streets looking up
and not have someone put her under a label?
Again, will she be able to walk the streets alone
and still reach home, safe and able?
And then I wonder about the things I can give her
if only I meet her half way.
And maybe talk to her, about her, for her,
until she finally gets a say.

#73

Maybe laughter is
your soul learning to fly
when all of its life
it's been told
to hold the wings in.

#74

And how
will
you know
of what
heals you
until
you know
of what
hurts?

75

Sometimes people change and
become a shadow of what we
knew. We try to break in to
find some sliver of the person
that existed before but all
we find are shutters and locks
in all the places we once
thought familiar to us. Where
do they go? I wonder. Where
do they hide their older
selves? Can we find them again?
And what would we say? I'm
sorry please come back though
I'm not sure
what I am sorry for.

76

I am going to be
whoever you need me to be.
If you need a friend
I will be that friend.
If you need a stranger
to mend your heart
for a bit and then be
on their way, then
I will be that stranger.
If you need a lover,
then I will let my words
speak to you of love.
You are loved.
You have a friend.
You are not alone.

Look into the mirror.
Repeat these words.

Sometimes
when people leave
they take their version of us
with them
leaving us free
to find ourselves again.

He who is broken
will be the one
most readily found
walking around fixing
the shattered windows
of your soul
for he knows too well
the feeling
of coming home
to a damaged house
and finding no corner
warm enough to sit in.

I wish I could help you,
console you,
tell you that it is okay to break into my arms,
that the world says you, man, must be stone,
but I will hide you if need be,
if you are afraid to be seen as water,
I will give you a corner of my heart
to lie and rest in,
to b r e a k i n t o w a v e s and cry in.
Men must not seem weak, they say,
but do you know emotion is strength?
My shoulders aren't as broad as yours
but they may give you a little reprieve
if you just lean your head for a while.
My arms may not be as strong, but they
will still find their way around you,
they can still surround you,
and keep you from falling.
Shatter if you want, but let me hold the pieces.
And when you are ready,
we will build you back again.

#80

Maybe moving on
is your heart forgiving you
for all the times you hurt it
because of them.

81

I know, you feel right now that it's not going to be okay.
That you will not be able to break these shackles
that are weighing you down. That life will not get better.
But it will.
You stood up before, didn't you?
You stood up when you thought you would never stand.
You made it. And you will make it again.
Remember there is nothing that can break you so badly,
that you will not be able to pull yourself together again.
You have been to the bottom, and from there you have
been trying to climb up.
And sometimes you slipped and fell a few steps back,
but you have held on. And that is all I am asking you
to do right now.

Hold
On.

Because you hide your fire inside
and do not let it grow
in fear of what people will see
and what they will know,
it will turn your breath to smoke
and finally go dim
but not before it burns
and kills everything within.

Why do you stay so quiet woman?
I watch flames dance within your eyes
when you are bursting to let your emotions run.
Why do you bite your tongue and walk away?
If your voice is music, your rage is thunder,
and maybe this world needs a little shaking,
a little waking up, a little breaking,
and then you build it, the way you want to.

#84

I say my spirit is restless
and you assume it
as a yearning of mine
to find an anchor.
But it is not.
It is a quality and I proclaim it.
I am restless,
I am wild,
I was born to be free.

85

Do not call her shy. For she is not.
She is quiet, for she reserves herself
for those who truly know her worth.
She derives energy from nature,
from solitude and passion, and the
slow reflection of life.
Love her, but more than that, listen.
Spend time observing her silent movements,
the tiny emotions that sometimes slip
through her calm facade. She will not speak
of most of it. To read her eyes, is to read
her soul. And to read both, one must
learn the language.

#86

I saw a black bird today
perched atop the tree in front of my house
and I wanted it to fly away.
Black is considered ominous where I come from.
But then it flew down and sat on my porch
and suddenly the black wasn't black anymore
but a range of blues and greens hiding
in the midst of black wings.
And I felt like a fool.
I'm sorry little bird. I whispered.
Society taught us to judge by the cover.
And so I judged and have been judged.
Not realizing that it is really them and me
who have our hearts tainted with black.
And we walk along proudly,
with painted faces and polished skins
knowing no one will ever look inside.

87

Let's be children again.
Let's lose ourselves in the longing
for summer, for christmas, santa
and chocolates. Let's know that
we'll be protected just by the
holding of a hand and fall asleep
the moment our heads find a warm
lap. Let's be free, as free as we
can be, and dream because our
whole life is in front of us and we
can carve it into what we need it to be.
Let's grow, and have our eyes filled
with wonder. Let's run as fast as we can
without measuring our steps or our pulse,
just for the joy of it, and laugh
because why shouldn't we?
Let's make our seasons spring again,
looking on to an endless summer..

88

I wonder where the fairies go
when they get tired of sprinkling
the world with fairy dust,
when all of their sparkle has been
given away. Isn't that what we all
are afraid of? Giving away
too much, receiving too little.
Folklore says, it is not the sparkle,
but the belief in the fairy which
makes it stronger. Would that be
the same case with us too?
Knowing that someone believes
in goodness, in hope, in humanity,
because of you. Is that not worth
giving some of your sparkle away?

#89

It takes courage to live,
to stand up and say that
this is what you believe in,
even if it comes out as a
whisper, even if you speak
of it in the dead of the night
when there is no one else
to hear it, even if you say it
to yourself for the first time.

#90

You thought you wouldn't get up, didn't you?
You thought the world was slipping away
from between your fingers and all you could do
was watch it go. And you felt uncertain, and helpless,
and rooted to the floor, your doubts gnawing at
your edges, telling you that you'll never be good enough.
But then something happened.
The world turned away from you, and you had
no one to talk to but yourself. And you found
out that it had a lot to say, a lot to show you,
and the purpose that you had been craving for, had
been seeking for so long, the solace, it was
all hiding within.
And you wept. You wept because it took twenty five
years for you to find you, to bring comfort
and understanding to your soul. And slowly you
became one with yourself. You stood up.
And then no one and nothing else mattered.

91

I have a feeling
that she does not
belong to the earth,
that every time she
sits with people
she finds herself
slipping away.
As though, there
are threads
tugging her out
to the stars.
Sometimes
I watch her leave
even without
her leaving the room,
and I know she is
where she needs to be.

#92

There was once a girl who decided to go to the moon
and not come back, for the earth was too banal,
too tight in all its customs,
not letting one enjoy madness of any kind,
any breath of fresh air manifest itself into the seasons.
And they just kept on repeating.
Spring, summer, autumn, winter.
What if she wanted blooms in her winter, and snowflakes in the
sun?
And all that cotton candy in the sky, with the most amazing shapes.
These people called them clouds.
Such a sad name for something so majestic, so dynamic and volatile,
blowing away in one moment, breaking open in the very next.
It seemed these people had such simple names
for everything beautiful,
everything to be preserved, nurtured and cherished.
She wished they would bring the big names back somehow.
Maybe the people would give more attention then.
But who knows when that would happen.
And so, s h e w e n t to t h e m o o n ,
sat gazing at earth from afar,
and made her own names for all that she had fallen in love with,
and no one there called her mad for it.

Thank you for reading Dear Dreamer.

If you liked the book and have a minute to spare, I would really appreciate a short review on the page or site where you bought the book. Reviews from readers like you make a huge difference to helping new readers find poetry like mine.

Your help in spreading the word is greatly appreciated.

Other books by Nihar Sharma

Wanderings

Author's Note

I wrote this book because I wish I had read it when I was a young girl, constantly in the need of approval and a sense of belonging. I still have those needs some days, but now I know that I am capable of fulfilling them.

And that is the message I hope to bring to you, dear dreamer. You are capable. You are enough.

Acknowledgment

I would like to express my gratitude to the very many introverts like me, who motivate me every day to accept and celebrate myself. Whether I have found you through social media, or books, or my everyday life, I thank you from the deepest reaches of my heart. This book is from you, to you.
I would also like to thank my adorable extrovert husband, for helping me stay grounded and focused. Your faith in my work genuinely surprises me every day.

About The Author

Nihar Sharma is an author of two collections of poetry, and she regularly writes and shares her work on social media under her alias 'The Dreamer', read by followers from across the globe. She is a native of Jammu, India, and currently resides in Kansas, US. When she's not writing, she's most likely reading, daydreaming or shooing off the squirrel from her bird feeder.

You can read more of her work at –
SharmaNihar.com
Facebook: Facebook.com/thedreamerdiary
Instagram: @thedream_diary
Twitter: @thedream_diary

CPSIA information can be obtained
at www.ICGtesting.com
Printed in the USA
LVHW042133231219
641445LV00003B/338/P